LEADING FROM WITHIN

Barry Nembhard

Leading from Within

Published by Spines

ISBN: 979-8-89383-107-8

LEADING FROM WITHIN

BARRY NEMBHARD

DEDICATION

This book is dedicated to my Mother, a true entrepreneurial inspiration I have ever known, and the heartwarming cornerstone known affectionately as Gwen, Mother, Mom by her cherished friends and family. Her unwavering spirit continues to illuminate our journey and ignite our entrepreneurial dreams.

CONTENTS

CHAPTER 1
LEADERSHIP

Every team, every organization and every company need leadership. With leadership, building structures and meeting commitments to customers or partners is easier.

The leadership culture is also crucial for the success or failure of individual teams or the entire company. It influences individual teams' motivation, willingness to work, and mood. However, for many people, leadership is still a very abstract concept.

What is the leadership definition?

The term leadership is more challenging to define than one might initially think. According to the business dictionary, leadership means "the orientation of the actions of individuals and groups towards the realization of predetermined goals, mediated through interaction" — a very abstract and not very concrete definition. Nevertheless, it offers a good starting point for determining good leadership. If we look at this definition, one might think that leadership is only designed to achieve company or sales goals. We should all be aware that this idea has been outdated for years.

There are numerous other points that good leadership should influence. Of course, the overarching goal of leadership – as the business dictionary definition correctly says – is to increase entrepreneurial success. At the same time, however, there are numerous smaller goals that leadership should achieve on the way to greater entrepreneurial success. This includes, for example, employee satisfaction, motivation and the development of structures that can lead to entrepreneurial success.

WHY IS LEADERSHIP SO IMPORTANT IN AN ORGANIZATION

There are two big and important reasons why leadership is such an important factor in every organization and company: the employer's attractiveness and the employees' motivation. You've probably heard the statement, "Employees don't leave the company; they leave leaders." This statement is one of the most important findings of our time. After all, it is not the company that influences employees daily and gives them tasks and structures, but rather the immediate leader. The leader is responsible for how well work processes work in the team, how the individual members interact, and whether they all pursue the same goals and pull together. Of course, some factors also depend on the team members, their motivation and attitude - but it is still the leader's responsibility to create a team that pursues common goals.

The better leadership works in a team or company, the happier and more motivated the teams are. This motivation ensures, on the one hand, that the employer's attractiveness to future applicants can be increased and, on the other hand, that better work results are achieved. A direct relationship has been proven between motivation and productivity or success of individual employees and entire teams: the more motivated the employee, the better the work results. In addition, motivated employees remain loyal to their employer in the long term.

The five most important tasks of leaders

At first glance, functional or indirect leadership sounds like an abstract definition of employee leadership.

Now, you will discover what specific tasks lie behind today's leadership.

Communicate goals and visions:

As we already mentioned in our definition of people management, teams need goals and visions to work together. It is up to leaders to develop these goals with employees and continually work towards them.

Promote and maintain motivation:

The more motivated each individual team member is, the more successfully they work and lead the team to greater success. In order to promote this motivation, communication, feedback, and a good dose of people's knowledge are necessary. Every employee is motivated by individual factors - these need to be discovered and addressed specifically. These can be, for example, financial incentives, compensatory time, subsidies for retirement provision or further training measures.

Provide support and structure:

Today's working world quickly seems unstructured for many people. The numerous technical developments and abstract tasks mean that there needs to be more structure in some areas. Leaders should ensure that these structures are created and function. Every team member should know what they are responsible for, what responsibilities there are and what topics can also be passed on to colleagues. Those who know their place in the team and are happy with it work more motivated.

Be an authentic role model:

This leadership task is the most difficult for most leaders. Employee management is not just about creating goals and structures for employees but also about adhering to the defined values. This includes making decisions in the interests of the team and modelling the way of working and communication that the team should also use. Ultimately, the leader is also seen as a role model.

Promote communication:

Communication in teams is a particularly important factor for the success of their collaboration. This not only includes regular feedback rounds with the entire team and each individual employee but also mediation in the event of conflicts. These cannot be avoided in any team. However, it is up to the leader to resolve the conflicts professionally and bring both sides back together.

BECOMING A LEADER – THESE QUALIFICATIONS ARE NEEDED FOR GOOD LEADERSHIP

There are now numerous courses that specifically prepare students for management roles in companies. In addition, many companies have mentoring programs or a program for young leaders to prepare them for their future tasks. However, it often happens that employees with excellent technical qualifications are promoted to leaders. This situation can quickly lead to problems without appropriate training - because only some specialists are good leaders. There is often a need for communicative skills or organizational skills. After all, the job of leaders is completely different from that of the executing team members.

These qualities are important for leaders

- Authentic
- Consequent
- Strong in communication
- Constructive
- Focused
- Trustworthy
- Appreciative
- Carefully
- Thinking systemically

Leaders need these leadership skills

- Strategic thinking
- Define and communicate goals
- Initiate and accompany changes
- Build and expand networks
- Prioritize and make decisions
- Knowledge of human nature
- Manage and resolve conflicts
- Leadership at a distance

Five tools that make good leadership easier

Even if there are no generally applicable instructions for employee management, leaders can use numerous empirical values as a guide and exchange ideas with other leaders and employees to find out exactly how their team can best be motivated. The principle clearly applies here: Communication is key. In order to find the right leadership style and become successful in leadership, there are some tools that leaders can use to develop and improve.

Tool 1: Employee interviews

One of the most important tools in employee management, if not the most important, is communication. Communication with the team, distribution of tasks, Feedback and development discussions are important cornerstones for the success of a leader. Regular employee discussions are particularly important. This can be a short feedback session after completing a part of the project, but also a detailed discussion regarding the goals and developments of each employee. Leaders should know what goals their employees pursue and what they do to achieve these goals. Leaders should find out about this in regular employee reviews. At the same time, such discussions allow you to give feedback in a calm atmosphere.

Tool 2: Conflict management

Conflict management is one of the most important tasks of leaders. Conflicts arise when different people come together. This is completely normal and often beneficial for productivity and motivation. However, it is important to deal with existing and emerging conflicts professionally. This is where leaders come into play. Employees have different opinions and are therefore restricted in the progress of their projects. However, conflicts can also arise between employees and customers that need to be resolved. The leader can act as a neutral mediator or, in complex cases, work with an external coach.

Tool 3: Employee development & team development

Both each individual employee and the entire team should develop further over time - supported by leaders. The task is, therefore, to use measures for employee and team development as a tool in employee management.

This specifically includes the development of professional goals with individual team members and support in achieving these goals through targeted support in the form of further training or coaching. At the same time, entire teams should reflect regularly: What is already going well for us and what is not yet? What can we do to improve further? This is possible through discussion groups or externally supervised workshops that take place regularly, for example, once a year.

Tool 4: Self-management

Another important tool for leaders is professional self-management. If you organize yourself well, set goals and work towards achieving them, you can also transfer these structures to the team. The topic of self-management or self-organization primarily includes tasks such as structuring working methods and creating structures and processes. In concrete terms, this means, for example, working with an organizational program that the entire team can access instead of having every employee work with classic to-do lists on paper. In this way, the productivity and motivation of team members can be gradually increased.

Tool 5: Communication training

Communication is the main task when it comes to good leadership. Inexperienced leaders, in particular, often need help at this point. How much information do employees really need? When do I give them too many details that they don't even need? How should problems and praise be communicated? These concerns are all too understandable - after all, it's not just what the leader says that matters, but more importantly, how they say it. However, proper communication is something that takes some practice. There are numerous communication training courses that have been developed specifically for leaders. Such training is also available for entire teams - so every team member can learn to communicate correctly on a professional level.

PRACTICAL TIP ON WHAT GOOD LEADERSHIP CAN LOOK LIKE

In addition to the theoretical content on the topic of good leadership, we would like to give you a few tips on how you can specifically implement good leadership.

Be a coach for your employees.

As a leader, you are not just there to manage the team. In addition to organizing projects, meetings or feedback discussions, there are a number of tasks, particularly on an interpersonal level - see yourself as a coach for your team. Your goal as a coach is to motivate each individual team member to perform at their best - and maintain their satisfaction. Address the problems, concerns and successes of your employees, provide support and offer assistance and look for goals and solutions to problems together with your team.

Create trust in the team.

Good teamwork depends heavily on the working atmosphere and the interpersonal situation in the team. If team members get along well with each other and know that they can rely on their colleagues, they feel safe and less stressed. If there are open conflicts or disagreements between team members, this can not only affect the working atmosphere but also the productivity of the team. This makes it all the more important to create trust in the team.

Bring your team together and create an atmosphere in which no one is afraid to speak up, contribute ideas or criticize.

Avoid micromanagement.

One of the biggest challenges for many leaders is avoiding micromanagement - many leaders have the understandable need to be informed about every step their employees take and to be able to give feedback on every step of the work. After all, you are the leader. However, you can tell only some employees what they have to do. Leave room for employees to develop freely, ensure that your team becomes independent thinkers and equip them with the necessary knowledge and tools.

Listen and communicate professionally.

We cannot emphasize it often enough: communication is a particularly important factor when it comes to good leadership. Work transparently, communicate openly with your team and give feedback. Also, listen to your team - learn to take important information with you and be reliable when someone asks you for help. By leading effectively, you not only earn the trust of your team, but you also inspire them to perform better. Another important tip: accept criticism. You are only human and can make mistakes - just like your team.

Develop visions and goals.

Developing specific goals is also part of your tasks as a leader. Sit down with your team and work out the goals you want to achieve, possible ways to get there and specific values and working methods that you would like to be guided by. This makes sense, for example, at the beginning of a project with agile methods such as Design Thinking or Business Canvas.

Learn self-management.

First and foremost, in order to manage a team, you must be able to manage yourself. Organize and structure your work. Try out different working methods and find the ones that best suit your way of working. These can be extensive to-do lists, calendars or productivity methods

like the Pomodoro Technique. If you are organized and structured yourself, you can, on the one hand, pass on the necessary tools to your employees and, on the other hand, set a good role model.

Learn to decide.

As a leader, you cannot avoid making uncomfortable decisions - or making decisions at all. Sometimes, there is no one right path - but a decision must be made as to which path to take. This decision is usually the responsibility of the leader. Learn to analyze the situation and make a decision based on in-depth knowledge.

Stay fit in your field.

Even if your main tasks now lie in the area of employee management, don't lose sight of your original area of expertise. This is the only way you can still assess how good your team's work is, where there is room for improvement and in which areas things are already going well. You also need to be good at customer communication - here, too, it is a good idea if you are familiar with the basic technical topics and are as up-to-date as possible.

Support the development of your team members.

Team development and people development are two topics that should be on every leader's to-do list. Through joint activities such as after-work events, trips to the laser tag arena or other sporting events, you can strengthen team spirit and bonds among employees. These measures are particularly worthwhile when someone new joins the team. In addition, every single employee should be given the opportunity for further training in order to achieve professional goals.

CONCLUSION: GOOD LEADERSHIP CAN BE LEARNED

Good leadership is still an abstract topic - that is likely to stay the same in the next few years. Every company, every team and every employee is different. Employee management must also adapt accordingly. Nevertheless, there are some basic principles that all leaders can and should follow. This makes it possible to learn good leadership skills and lead teams in such a way that they not only help the company to be more successful but are also satisfied and

see meaning in their task. Because that's what the modern working world is increasingly about, the work that you spend so much of your life doing should have meaning.

CHAPTER 2
LEADERSHIP THEORIES & LEADERSHIP STYLES

Leadership describes an extensive process that is influenced by many factors - starting with the leader, i.e., a superior and the organization itself, through those being led (employees or colleagues) to external influences from the environment. In order to better reflect the complexity of this process, various leadership theories have been developed within social and business research. Leadership theories include:

Trait approach:

Successful leadership depends primarily on the personality of the leader and their characteristics.

Behavioral approach:

Leadership style plays a major role here. For example, a distinction is made between an authoritarian and cooperative leadership style and between a person-oriented and task-oriented leadership style.

Situational approach:

This type of leadership is based on the respective situation. The actions and behavior of the leader are, therefore, based, for example, on the circumstances of interpersonal relationships or the existing task structure.

Interaction approach:

With this form of leadership, all people involved in the leadership process, as well as the situational context, are taken into account. What is particularly relevant is the interaction of various factors.

Systemic leadership:

This approach primarily takes into account the interaction between leaders and employees in the sense of networks but also influencing factors outside an organization.

Personal systems approach:

It is based on the findings of cybernetics or systems theory, according to which a leader controls those being led by using appropriate instruments and taking into account situational factors and goals in such a way that leadership success can be achieved.

LEADERSHIP STYLES

Based on the various leadership theories, corresponding leadership styles were defined. These primarily describe the way in which leaders treat their subordinates within a company. A leadership style describes the basic attitude of a leader, how and with what means the achievement of goals is ensured. Based on this attitude, it is also determined which activities are defined as management tasks and must be carried out by the superior.

1. Autocratic leadership style

The autocratic leadership style is expressed in the unlimited authority of the superior. A strict hierarchy forms the basic building block for such actions. Within this leadership style, decisions can be made quickly and without compromise, which is particularly advantageous in crisis situations such as those in the military or police. However, this leadership style is rarely practiced today.

Example: You and your team have a task to complete. With the autocratic leadership style, your boss tells you exactly what the goal is and how you have to proceed to achieve it.

Advantages

1. Decisions are made quickly.
2. Clear instructions and clear hierarchical structures
3. Employees have fewer responsibilities and only have to complete their assigned tasks.
4. Responsibilities are clearly clarified.

Disadvantages

1. Less motivated employees because they cannot contribute.
2. Unhealthy working atmosphere
3. Outdated model
4. Employees' innovative ideas are lost.
5. A lot of work for the superiors

2. Authoritarian leadership style

The authoritarian leadership style is based on the delegation of tasks by the person in the leadership role to those being led. There are only minor differences to the autocratic leadership style. The authority of the leader, especially in decisions, is very high. As a result, there is no co-determination within the organization on the part of those led.

Example: Nowadays, this leadership style is mainly found in the police, the Bundeswehr,

or the fire department, where hierarchy plays a major role and is delegated accordingly from above.

Advantages:

1. Quick decision making
2. Clear distribution of tasks
3. High level of control

Disadvantages:

1. Little flexibility
2. No room for creativity and innovation
3. Sole responsibility lies with the manager

3. Bureaucratic leadership style

Rules come first in the bureaucratic leadership style, which is why it is also a form of authoritarian leadership style. Key features are the clearly defined rules and regulations that govern both work processes and changes to them, the limited influence of the leader and potentially lengthy decision-making processes. This leadership style ensures that employees adhere to the rules and, at the same time, relieves the burden on leaders by minimizing responsibility. However, this style could be more flexible.

The bureaucratic leadership style is popular in administrations; for example, you are given precise time-lines and plans for how you and your team must complete a task. You then have to stick to this strictly.

Advantages

1. Clear work instructions and responsibilities
2. Regulated workflows
3. Fewer wrong decisions
4. Decisions are made based on guidelines and not on sympathy, gut feeling or one's own opinion.

Disadvantages

1. No room for innovation and new ideas
2. Long decision-making processes and little scope for decision-making
3. No flexible structures
4. Demotivated leaders and employees

4. Charismatic leadership style

In the charismatic leadership style, the focus is on the charisma of the superior. Because of her charisma, she is in the leadership role. One consequence is identification with the leader and often with the resulting brand. While there is no concrete say on the part of those being led, they are motivated by the leader.

This leadership style is used in companies with identical founders and managing directors, such as Apple and Steve Jobs.

Advantages

1. High motivation and willingness to perform among employees
2. Higher loyalty of employees to the company and thus a lower fluctuation rate
3. The employees identify with the company's goals and visions

Disadvantages

1. Only works if the boss has the right personality.
2. Employees who are easy to convince are more likely to be exploited.

5. Democratic leadership style

The communication of employees' input or suggestions is specifically encouraged by superiors in a democratic leadership style. The goal is to actively involve all employees. Everyone involved has equal rights, and decisions cannot be made by superiors alone. Greater appreciation within the organization but also a greater degree of required discipline and order arise in this leadership style.

The democratic leadership style is particularly practised in companies with extremely qualified employees.

Example: With a cooperative leadership style, you, your team, and your leader discuss together how you can best accomplish a task. Each of you brings your own ideas and opinions

- Especially different and opposing opinions are welcome.

Advantages

- Relief for leaders because they do not make all decisions alone.
- Higher employee motivation
- Greater sense of responsibility among employees
- Promoting personal initiative, creativity and innovation
- Avoiding wrong decisions
- Higher engagement and commitment from employees

Disadvantages

- Loss of control and bad decisions when superiors cannot assert themselves or lose track of things.
- Longer decision-making processes through discussions and many different opinions
- Greater competitiveness among employees

6. Laissez-faire leadership style

If you learned French at school, you will know that the laissez-faire management style gives employees the greatest freedom. The French term "laissez-faire" literally means "let things happen," and bosses who apply this principle give their teams a lot of leeway to make their own decisions.

The laissez-faire leadership style gives employees more decision-making power because employees work as they see fit. However, there is a risk that too little intervention will inhibit the professional development of your workforce and waste important opportunities for the company's growth. Therefore, not using this leadership style without some control is important.

Example: A new project with clear tasks and goals is created. The teams organize themselves, and the responsibilities and approaches are left to everyone.

Advantages:

1. Supports creativity and innovation
2. Promotes self-motivation and self-realization

Disadvantages:

1. Requires a high level of specialist knowledge.
2. The feeling of insecurity among employees due to unclear expectations
3. Danger of competitiveness and bullying

7. Transactional leadership

The transactional leadership style emphasizes control, organization, short-term planning, and the use of rewards and punishments to motivate employees.

Transactional and autocratic leadership have many similarities, but the key difference is that transactional leadership involves clear communication between the leader and team members.

In return for complying with regulations and providing high performance, an employee can, for example, be rewarded with a promotion.

Advantages

1. It can be an efficient way to achieve short-term goals.

2. Clearly defines the behavior expected of team members through a system of rewards and punishments.
3. Provides structure and stability.

Disadvantages

1. Limits creativity, growth and initiative.
2. May have no effect on people who are not driven by extrinsic motivation.
3. It can be daunting for individuals seeking professional and personal development opportunities.

8. Transformational leadership

By creating a vision based on identified needs and directing their teams towards a common objective, transformational leaders inspire and motivate their teams.

The major difference between transformational leadership and the other leadership styles discussed so far is that it focuses on changing systems and processes that need to be fixed, in contrast to transactional or bureaucratic leadership, which does not aim to change the status quo.

Advantages

1. Motivating the team

2. Promotes building strong relationships and encourages collaboration.
3. Gives team members autonomy to get their work done.
4. It can lead to greater creativity, growth and empathy in the team.

Disadvantages

1. May not be the best fit for certain organizations (e.g. bureaucratic).
2. May cause feelings of instability and disrupt the status quo.
3. High pressure on the leader, who has to lead by example.

9. Participative leadership style

The participative leadership style is one of the forms of leadership that Lewin defined. This leadership style focuses on a combination of cooperative and authoritarian leadership styles. Because supervisors often need to apply a leadership style in its purest form in everyday working life. A participatory management style involves employees in company operations and decision-making. However, the level of participation is limited. In contrast to the cooperative management style, in which employees are involved in all decisions, there are limitations here.

Nevertheless, attractive models are offered to employees within the participative leadership style. These are, for example, a company pension plan, a company canteen or benefits in kind or corporate benefits. In this way, the company tries to bind its employees more closely.

10. Meaning-oriented leadership

Meaning-oriented leadership is based on the philosophical approach that the pursuit of meaning is a person's highest motivation. If employees do not understand the meaning of a job or task, they refuse and have to be strongly influenced. Because of this, the leader must communicate the purpose of the tasks and build loyalty and trust.

Just like direction-oriented leadership, this leadership style can also be used in all organizations.

11. Personality-oriented leadership

Personality-oriented leadership is considered a continuation of situational leadership. In this leadership style, the individual personalities of the employees are also taken into account. The aim is that these can be used and influenced individually in order to achieve leadership success ultimately. Based on the employee's personality type, the leader chooses communication channels and choice of words and delegates appropriate tasks. This increases appreciation and loyalty significantly.

12. Coaching leadership

Coaching leadership is a leadership style characterized by collaboration, support and guidance. Coaching leaders focus on getting the best out of their teams by guiding them through goals and obstacles.

Advantages

1. Encourages mutual communication and collaboration.
2. Includes a lot of constructive feedback.
3. Facilitates the personal and professional development of the individual.
4. The focus is on support, not judgment.
5. Creates opportunities for growth and creative thinking.

Disadvantages

1. Resource-intensive because it takes a lot of time and effort.
2. Doesn't always yield the quickest and most effective results.
3. Might not be the best option for high-pressure or strictly results-oriented companies.

13. Situational leadership

Situational leadership takes into account the situation

as well as the professional and psychological abilities of each employee in order to find the right leadership style. Supervisors must, therefore, evaluate each situation individually before they can act. This is how communication channels, choice of words and much more are chosen.

Situational leadership can basically be used in all organizations. Nevertheless, the number of employees to be managed should be manageable so that an effective evaluation can take place.

This results in the four levels of situational leadership:

Maturity level 1 – Dictation: As the boss, you give precise instructions to an inexperienced employee and control the work processes and performance. This enables you to quickly notice and fix mistakes brought on by a lack of specialized knowledge. In addition, clear guidelines help an inexperienced employee not to feel lost.

Maturity level 2 – Training: Now, the experienced employee has the chance to practice the skills they have learned. You, as the boss, give him more freedom to try things out and act more independently. It can have a very motivating effect on the employee when he realizes that he is being trusted. Of course, the leader should still be there to support the employee and give them the opportunity to clarify questions.

Maturity level 3 – Participate: The employee now has more experience, and their skills are more developed. That's why his independence continues to grow. That's why you can increase his scope for decision-making. You are now actively motivating the employee to make their own decisions.

Maturity level 4 – Delegating: At this level, the employee is technically competent and knows their work very well. As a leader, you hardly have to intervene anymore. This allows you to hand over responsibility for decision-making and implementation to the employee.

You can divide the situational leadership style into two types of leadership – the direction-related leadership style and the group-related leadership style:

Direction-oriented leadership

Directional leadership describes the potential paths that superiors can take to achieve goals. A distinction is made here between the fact-oriented and the person-oriented path. While the superiors in the fact-oriented path exert pressure to perform and completing tasks is the first priority, the superiors in the person-oriented path rely on personal relationships with employees and see themselves as their partners.

Group-oriented leadership style

The group-oriented leadership style forms a situational style. The superior treats the subordinates differently depending on the situation and their needs in order to be responsible for group success. In this way, the leader integrates new members into the group or encourages members when their motivation is low.

The group-oriented leadership style is particularly suitable when working in larger groups such as production teams or marketing teams.

WHY ARE LEADERSHIP STYLES SO IMPORTANT?

The respective leadership style can have a very big influence on the success of the company. Especially in today's world, when issues such as the shortage of skilled workers are becoming increasingly important, companies should be careful when choosing the type of management. Because if employees are managed optimally, this can have a positive effect on satisfaction, motivation and commitment. And of course, this also has a major influence on customer satisfaction and ideal cooperation with various business partners.

There are some empirical studies that have shown that a well-managed company is also more economically successful. Higher growth rates and returns are achieved. Of course, many entrepreneurs are now wondering which leadership style is best. However, this depends heavily on what goal is to be achieved. For example, should the focus be on promoting young talent, job satisfaction or organizational performance?

CONCLUSION

Depending on which goal is selected, the appropriate leadership style should ultimately be tailored to it. Various empirical studies have shown that discussion leadership styles can have a very positive effect on a company. Success can arise particularly with regard to various organizational performance indicators, such as team performance or job satisfaction.

Of course, leadership behavior also plays a central role in the chances of success. As a result, ideal personnel and management development should be addressed in a company. A combination of training and feedback should form the framework for this development measure.

CHAPTER 3
DIFFERENT PERSPECTIVES OF LEADERSHIP

There are different angles and perspectives on leading people, as the following figure shows. Some of them are unusual but still very crucial when it comes to successful collaboration and careers.

Key perspectives on leadership are:

As a rule, leadership in organizations is understood as downward leadership, as the leadership of subordinate employees. This perspective of leadership in the narrower sense is certainly the classic and obvious one on the topic of leadership. Companies usually invest in training and leadership development without reservations and expect their leaders to expand these skills further. The connection with operational success seems clear; after all, leaders want to implement the goals from above among their employees through influence. As a matter of course, leadership training usually only conveys this perspective.

Upward leadership

Upward leadership is the leadership with which employees direct and direct their superiors. For the individual leader, this may be the most important aspect of leadership, as careers and aspects of self-realization depend very much on this competence. A lot depends on this: "Do I get the green light and tailwind for my projects?" "Do I get enough employees, finances and other resources for my area of responsibility?". Anyone who can lead upwards and convince people can achieve much more in companies - and they can also move better in terms of their careers.

The interest in this topic among individual leaders should, therefore, be high. In fact, many leaders are often even more concerned with this than with downward leadership. It is, therefore, surprising that there are so far few publications and training offers for leaders on upward leadership. However, the willingness of employers to invest in such skills is understandably rather low because the idea that management is from the bottom up usually contradicts the usual thinking and self-image of decision-makers.

Lateral leadership

There is also the term lateral leadership, which is defined as the leadership of people with equal hierarchical status. Lateral leadership is often required to complete projects successfully. Anyone who fails to work well together on one level and forge alliances will have disadvantages as a leader. Although this is an essential aspect for the practical success of a department for which a leader is responsible, there is hardly any approach to this in training courses and textbooks.

An important leadership perspective also lies in the interaction with external groups such as customers and other interaction partners (e.g., suppliers or service providers). Only those who understand how to steer the behavior of these relatively independent groups in the desired direction can actually act successfully as a leader.

Self-leadership

Self-leadership is an essential leadership skill. This ability is a prerequisite for leading other people. Anyone who is not suitable as a role model has no goals or cannot achieve their goals in a systematic and organized manner will find it difficult to find acceptance and success as a leader. A sentence from Nietzsche captures this finding well: "He is commanded who cannot obey himself." In addition, this area also includes the successful "balance" (better integration) and organization of private life, work and regeneration phases. This is also a basic requirement for high performance as a leader.

DIFFERENCE BETWEEN LEADERSHIP AND MANAGEMENT

Is there a difference between leadership and management? It is not uncommon for the terms leadership and management to be equated or confused. This is not surprising, as different people understand leadership and management differently. On the other hand, it is obvious that there are leaders who do not lead - and there are people who lead but are not leaders (such as informal leaders). This section discusses the terms "management" and "leadership" and highlights possible differences.

Management

The term management is now used for everything, such as time management or self-management. Even the caretaker is now sometimes called a "facility leader." Management, in the narrower sense, refers to optimizing processes and structures in companies. Management in companies is used to optimize processes (such as sales processes) and structures (such as IT infrastructure). Management, therefore, has a lot to do with the principle of "doing things right!". This applies, for example, to aspects such as work and production processes, finances, infrastructure or technology - but also the employees. It isn't easy to imagine optimizing structures or processes without targeted influence on employees. The guide is also an important tool in management, probably the most important. Management, as a term for a group of high-ranking people, also relies on the formal authority of a position in order to exert influence.

Leadership

Leadership emphasizes influencing people and motivating and supporting employees and groups. A key difference to management is the exclusive focus on people and influencing them towards goals. Leadership has a lot to do with goals and the principle of "doing the

right thing!". In addition, unlike management, leadership is not tied to a formal position. It is not uncommon for people without formal responsibility to lead by strongly influencing the behavior and experiences of other people in organizations. In a sense, this characteristic makes leadership broader than "just" an important instrument of management.

Leadership characteristics

- Leadership is implemented within the framework of social systems and, therefore, results from the relationships between individuals.

- Leadership usually goes hand in hand with certain power hierarchies; that is, leadership involves asymmetrical relationships of superiority and subordination.
- Leadership is designed for a goal.
- Leadership applies to both individuals and groups.
- Leadership can be shared.
- Leadership is not formally tied to specific positions.

CONCLUSION

Leadership and management have different priorities and can complement each other very well. Since both terms are "vague," it ultimately depends on the subjective definitions whether one sees differences or not.

CHAPTER 4
THE ROLES OF A LEADER

In order for a leader to lead his team well and get the optimal results from the team, he must take on different roles. Depending on the situation, a different role is in the foreground - it doesn't matter which leadership style is involved.

You differentiate between the eight roles:

Facilitator:

The leader concentrates on collaborative interaction within the team. It promotes teamwork and tries to resolve conflicts through compromise.

Mediator:

But it's more than just the working atmosphere within the team that is important. As an intermediary, the boss also represents the team externally. He should pay attention to his appearance and try to convey his team's wishes to the outside world.

Mentor:

The leader should not only focus on the employees' work performance but also guide them as their mentor and promote their strengths. This also includes listening to them, showing empathy and understanding, and encouraging their ideas. In addition, supervisors usually have more professional experience than their employees. Employees can benefit from this knowledge.

Producer:

Of course, the performance of the employees is also significant. As a producer, the leader is very results-oriented. It motivates employees to exploit their performance potential and achieve better results.

Monitor:

In order to get the best out of the team, it is important to know the strengths and weaknesses of the employees. It is, therefore, necessary for leaders to regularly monitor performance. This is the only way to ensure long-term success for the team and the entire company.

Coordinator:

The leader is also responsible for keeping track of all upcoming tasks and for coordinating and organizing the projects.

Director:

As a director, you plan and manage the division of tasks. You should also pay attention to the strengths and weaknesses of your employees. You also set clear goals and discuss your expectations with your employees.

Innovator:

A leader should also bring new, creative ideas. Because only through changes can there be improvements. It also makes everyday working life more exciting.

CONCLUSION

Depending on the experience and personality of the employees and the team, the leader has to slip into different roles. Of course, it also depends on the personality and experience of the boss as to which of the eight roles works best and is appropriate in the situation.

CHAPTER 5
SELF-LEADERSHIP

The importance of self-leadership in the contemporary workplace and the many advantages it offers to people and organizations were discussed in the previous chapter. We will now go into greater detail about the idea of self-leadership, outlining what it entails and illuminating the complex connection between self-leadership and leadership. Additionally, we will explore why self-leadership is an indispensable foundation for effective leadership.

Understanding Self-Leadership

At its core, self-leadership is the practice of taking control of one's own behaviors, actions, and decisions to achieve personal and professional goals. It involves a high degree of self-awareness, self-motivation, and self-regulation. Self-leadership is not about managing others; rather, it is about managing oneself effectively and responsibly.

THE PILLARS OF SELF-LEADERSHIP

1. Self-Awareness:

Self-leadership begins with an acute understanding of oneself. This includes recognizing strengths, weaknesses, values, beliefs, and aspirations. Self-aware individuals are attuned to their emotions, motivations, and behaviors. They are able to recognize opportunities for development and can match their actions with their values and objectives.

2. Self-motivation:

Motivation is the driving force behind self-leadership. Self-motivated individuals have a clear sense of purpose and are driven by intrinsic factors. They set meaningful goals, maintain focus, and exhibit determination and perseverance in the pursuit of those goals. They do not rely solely on external rewards or incentives to stay motivated.

3. Self-Regulation:

Self-regulation involves the ability to manage one's impulses, emotions, and behaviors effectively. It includes controlling negative emotions, delaying gratification, and maintaining discipline. Self-regulated individuals are less likely to succumb to procrastination, impulsivity, or emotional reactivity.

4. Self-Development:

Self-leadership is synonymous with continuous self-improvement. Individuals who practice self-leadership invest in their personal and professional development. They seek opportunities for learning, acquire new skills, and adapt to changing circumstances. They view setbacks as opportunities for growth and resilience.

THE RELATIONSHIP BETWEEN SELF-LEADERSHIP AND LEADERSHIP

Self-leadership is the foundation upon which effective leadership is built. It forms the bedrock upon which leaders can develop and refine their leadership skills. Here's how self-leadership and leadership intersect:

1. Leading Oneself:

Leadership begins with leading oneself. Before one can lead others, one must demonstrate mastery over their own actions, behaviors, and emotions. Self-leadership enables leaders to set an example for the attitudes and behaviors they want from their teams. It serves as a powerful example for others to follow.

2. Leading by Example:

Leaders can model the attitudes and behaviors they want from their teams by practicing self-leadership. When team members see their leaders taking initiative, setting goals, and consistently delivering results, they are inspired to do the same. Leading by example is a hallmark of effective leadership.

3. Emotional Intelligence:

Self-leadership fosters emotional intelligence—an essential trait for effective leaders. Leaders with high emotional intelligence are able to comprehend, control, and relate to their own emotions as well as those of others. This skill enables leaders to build stronger relationships, resolve conflicts, and inspire their teams.

4. Decision-Making:

Self-leadership enhances decision-making skills. Leaders who practice self-leadership are adept at making informed and thoughtful decisions. They weigh risks, think about the long-term effects of their decisions, and make decisions that are consistent with the values and goals of the organization.

5. Adaptability:

Self-leadership equips leaders with the adaptability needed in today's rapidly changing world. Leaders who have mastered self-leadership can navigate uncertainty and guide their teams through transitions with resilience and confidence.

WHY SELF-LEADERSHIP IS ESSENTIAL FOR EFFECTIVE LEADERSHIP

The connection between self-leadership and effective leadership is inseparable. Those who want to be effective leaders must first learn to lead themselves for the following compelling reasons:

1. Authenticity

Self-leadership encourages authenticity. Leaders who practice self-leadership are more likely to be genuine, transparent, and true to themselves. Authentic leaders are trusted by their teams because they are perceived as honest and consistent in their actions and decisions.

2. Adaptability

In today's fast-paced world, leaders must be adaptable. Self-leadership fosters adaptability by instilling a growth mindset and a willingness to embrace change as an opportunity for growth. Leaders who are self-leaders are more likely to steer their teams through change effectively.

3. Emotional Intelligence

High emotional intelligence is necessary for effective leadership. Self-leadership is closely tied to emotional intelligence, as it involves understanding and managing one's emotions. Leaders who are emotionally intelligent can empathize with their team members, resolve conflicts, and foster a positive work environment.

4. Accountability

Accountability is a hallmark of effective leadership. Self-leadership encourages personal accountability, which sets the standard for accountability within a team or organization. Leaders who practice self-leadership take responsibility for their actions and outcomes, inspiring their teams to do the same.

5. Influence

Leaders who practice self-leadership are more influential. Their actions and behaviors serve as a powerful source of influence on their teams. Team members are more likely to respect and emulate leaders who demonstrate self-mastery and consistency.

6. Resilience

Leaders face adversity and challenges regularly. Self-leadership builds resilience, enabling leaders to bounce back from setbacks and setbacks. Resilient leaders can maintain composure, make rational decisions, and lead their teams through difficult times.

CONCLUSION

In this chapter, we have defined self-leadership as the practice of taking control of one's own behaviors, actions, and decisions. We have explored the pillars of self-leadership and the profound relationship between self-leadership and effective leadership. Additionally, we've delved into the compelling reasons why self-leadership is essential for anyone aspiring to lead effectively.

As we move forward in this journey to create a winning culture and lead teams, keep in mind that self-leadership is not an isolated concept; it is the cornerstone upon which effective leadership is built. In the chapters ahead, we will explore practical strategies and exercises to enhance your self-leadership skills, empowering you to lead with authenticity, resilience, and impact.

CHAPTER 6
THE SIGNIFICANCE OF SELF-LEADERSHIP IN TODAY'S WORLD

In the ever-evolving landscape of the modern workplace, leadership is no longer a trait reserved solely for those with titles and formal positions of authority.

The traditional top-down hierarchy has given way to a more dynamic and inclusive approach, where leadership transcends organizational charts and flows from within every individual. This fundamental shift in the perception of leadership has propelled the concept of self-leadership to the forefront of organizational success. In this chapter, we will delve into the profound importance of self-leadership in today's world and explore the myriad benefits that come with mastering this essential skill.

The Changing Face of Leadership

Gone are the days when leadership was synonymous with a corner office, a title, and a desk adorned with a nameplate. Today's organizations operate in a fast-paced, interconnected, and ever-changing environment. The rigid hierarchies of the past have given way to flatter structures, cross-functional teams, and a growing emphasis on collaboration and innovation. In this dynamic landscape, leadership is no longer confined to a select few but rather distributed across the entire organization.

Why has this shift occurred? The answer lies in the demands of the contemporary workplace. Rapid technological advancements, increased competition, and the need for agility have necessitated a new approach to leadership. Organizations require individuals who can take initiative, make decisions, adapt to change, and inspire others—qualities traditionally associated with leadership. This evolution has given rise to the concept of self-leadership, where every member of the organization is empowered to take ownership of their actions, decisions, and contributions.

THE ESSENCE OF SELF-LEADERSHIP

Self-leadership is not a newfangled term or a passing trend; it is a fundamental mindset and set of behaviors that are indispensable in the modern workplace. At its core, self-leadership encompasses the ability to take responsibility for one's actions, behaviors, and results. It involves setting clear goals, making informed decisions, and managing one's own development. Self-leadership also includes the capacity to adapt to change, persevere in the face of adversity, and continually strive for improvement.

One key aspect of self-leadership is self-awareness. It involves understanding one's strengths, weaknesses, values, and aspirations. Self-aware people can recognize their own blind spots and make conscious efforts to improve their abilities. They are attuned to their emotions and behaviors, enabling them to make choices that align with their personal and professional goals.

THE BENEFITS OF MASTERING SELF-LEADERSHIP

Now that we've explored the essence of self-leadership let's delve into the myriad benefits that come with mastering this skill. Self-leadership is not just a personal development buzzword; it is a transformative force that can positively impact individuals, teams, and entire organizations.

1. Enhanced Personal Effectiveness

At its core, self-leadership empowers individuals to become more effective in their roles. When employees take ownership of their work, set clear objectives, and prioritize their tasks, they become more productive and efficient. They can better manage their time, make informed decisions, and achieve their goals with greater precision.

2. Improved Decision-Making

Self-leadership fosters better decision-making. Self-leaders are more likely to weigh the advantages and disadvantages of various options, look for pertinent information, and make decisions that are consistent with their goals and core values. This results in sounder and more thoughtful decisions, benefiting both themselves and their organizations.

3. Increased Adaptability

Adaptability is a prized skill in a time of constant change and uncertainty. Self-leadership equips individuals with the resilience and flexibility needed to navigate change effectively. Those who master self-leadership are more likely to embrace change as an opportunity for growth rather than as a threat and can guide their teams through transitions with confidence.

4. Heightened Motivation and Engagement

Self-leadership is inherently tied to motivation and engagement. When individuals take ownership of their work and set meaningful goals, they feel a stronger sense of purpose and motivation. This increased drive leads to greater engagement, job satisfaction, and a willingness to go above and beyond.

5. Positive Influence on Teams

The benefits of self-leadership extend beyond the individual. When team members practice self-leadership, they become positive influencers within their teams. They lead by example, demonstrating the importance of accountability, adaptability, and proactive problem-solving. As a result, the team develops a culture of leadership in which everyone is accountable for the group's success.

6. Organizational Excellence

Ultimately, the mastery of self-leadership at the individual and team levels contributes to organizational excellence. Organizations that cultivate a culture of self-leadership are better equipped to adapt to change, innovate, and excel in their respective industries. They harness the collective leadership potential of their workforce, which, in turn, fuels continuous improvement and innovation.

CONCLUSION

As we embark on this journey of exploring self-leadership and its profound impact on today's organizations, it is crucial to recognize that leadership is not limited to titles or positions. Leadership begins with self-leadership—the ability to take charge of one's actions, behaviors, and results. By mastering self-leadership, individuals can enhance their personal effectiveness, make better decisions, adapt to change, and motivate themselves and their teams.

The benefits of self-leadership ripple through the organization, fostering a culture of excellence and empowerment. In the next chapters, we will delve deeper into the practical aspects of self-leadership and how it can be harnessed to create a winning culture and lead teams to new heights of success.

CHAPTER 7

THE CRUCIAL ROLE OF SELF-AWARENESS

In the journey to create a winning culture and lead teams effectively, one of the fundamental building blocks is self-leadership. As we've discussed in previous chapters, self-leadership is the practice of taking control of one's own behaviors, actions, and decisions. At the heart of self-leadership lies self-awareness—an indispensable quality that serves as the compass for effective leadership. In this chapter, we delve into the significance of self-awareness in self-leadership, explore techniques for increasing self-awareness, and discover the transformative role of mindfulness in enhancing our self-awareness.

The Cornerstone of Self-Leadership: Self-Awareness

Understanding Self-Awareness

Knowing oneself well means being able to identify and comprehend one's own thoughts, feelings, behaviors, strengths, weaknesses, values, and motivations. It is like holding up a mirror to oneself and gaining insight into one's inner workings. This profound self-understanding forms the foundation of self-leadership and effective leadership.

THE IMPORTANCE OF SELF-AWARENESS IN SELF-LEADERSHIP

1. Informed Decision-Making

Self-awareness equips individuals with the information needed to make informed decisions. When you are aware of your values, goals, and motivations, you can align your choices with your true desires. In self-leadership, this means setting goals that resonate with your values and making choices that support those goals.

2. Emotional Intelligence

Being able to recognize and understand one's own thoughts, feelings, behaviors, strengths, weaknesses, values, and motivations is the definition of knowing oneself well. Leaders with high emotional intelligence can navigate interpersonal dynamics effectively, foster positive relationships, and inspire trust among their team members.

3. Authentic Leadership

Authentic leadership is built on self-awareness. Authentic leaders are genuine, transparent, and true to themselves. They are comfortable with their strengths and vulnerabilities, which makes them relatable and trustworthy to their teams.

4. Adaptability

In times of change and uncertainty, self-awareness is the compass that guides leaders. It allows leaders to acknowledge their reactions to change, whether it's resistance, fear, or excitement, and respond in a way that aligns with their goals and values. Self-aware leaders are better equipped to adapt to changing circumstances.

5. Conflict Resolution

Conflicts are an inevitable part of any workplace. Self-awareness enables leaders to understand their own triggers and reactions in conflict situations. By recognizing their own biases and emotional responses, they can approach conflicts with objectivity and work towards resolutions.

TECHNIQUES FOR INCREASING SELF-AWARENESS

1. Journaling

A useful tool for introspection and self-discovery is journaling. Recording your thoughts, emotions, and experiences helps you identify patterns and gain insight into your inner world. You can use journaling to explore your values, set goals, and track your progress.

2. 360-Degree feedback

Seek feedback from colleagues, supervisors, and team members. A 360-degree feedback process provides you with a comprehensive view of how others perceive your strengths and areas for improvement. It can be an eye-opening experience that deepens your self-awareness.

3. Mindful Self-Reflection

Take time for mindful self-reflection. This involves setting aside moments of quiet and solitude to reflect on your thoughts and feelings without judgment. Mindfulness practices, which we will explore shortly, can be integrated into your self-reflection routine.

4. Personality Assessments

Tools like the Myers-Briggs Type Indicator (MBTI), StrengthsFinder, or the Enneagram can offer insights into your personality traits, strengths, and potential blind spots. These assessments serve as a starting point for self-awareness exploration.

5. Coaching and Mentoring

Engage in coaching or mentoring relationships where you can receive objective feedback and guidance from experienced individuals. A skilled coach or mentor can help you uncover blind spots and develop a deeper understanding of yourself.

THE ROLE OF MINDFULNESS IN SELF-AWARENESS

The practice of mindfulness entails being open and non-judgmental as you pay attention to the moment at hand. It can be a transformative tool for enhancing self-awareness in self-leadership. Here's how mindfulness contributes to self-awareness:

1. Emotion Regulation

Mindfulness allows you to observe your emotions as they arise without reacting impulsively. When faced with challenging situations, mindfulness helps you pause, acknowledge your emotions, and choose a measured response.

2. Increased Self-Observation

Through mindfulness, you become a keen observer of your thoughts, emotions, and bodily sensations. This heightened self-observation fosters greater self-awareness as you gain insight into your mental and emotional processes.

3. Reduction of Cognitive Distortions

Cognitive distortions—irrational thoughts that can cause negative emotions and behaviors—can be recognized and contested with the aid of mindfulness. By recognizing these distortions, you can replace them with more balanced and realistic thinking.

4. Enhanced Focus and Clarity

A regular mindfulness practice sharpens your focus and mental clarity. This mental clarity enables you to discern your goals, values, and priorities more clearly, contributing to greater self-awareness.

5. Stress Reduction

Mindfulness reduces stress by promoting relaxation and reducing the "fight or flight" response to stressors. A calm and relaxed mind is better equipped for self-reflection and self-awareness.

CONCLUSION

Self-awareness is the bedrock of self-leadership—a quality that is indispensable for effective leadership. It empowers leaders to make informed decisions, navigate emotions, build authentic relationships, adapt to change, and resolve conflicts. Techniques such as journaling, 360-

degree feedback, self-reflection, personality assessments, coaching, and mentoring can deepen your self-awareness.

Mindfulness, in particular, is a potent practice that enhances self-awareness by promoting emotional regulation, self-observation, clarity, and stress reduction. In the chapters ahead, we will explore how self-awareness, combined with other self-leadership skills, can help you create a winning culture and lead your teams to new heights of success.

CHAPTER 8
MASTERING SELF-REGULATION TO AID SELF-LEADERSHIP

In our exploration of self-leadership, we've learned about the foundational importance of self-awareness and how it serves as the compass guiding effective leadership. Now, we focus on another crucial self-leadership pillar—self-regulation. In this chapter, we will delve into self-regulation, explore techniques for improving self-regulation, and understand the indispensable role of self-discipline in mastering this essential skill.

Understanding Self-Regulation
Defining Self-Regulation

Self-regulation, in the context of self-leadership, refers to effectively managing one's impulses, emotions, and behaviors. It is the capacity to control oneself, even in challenging situations or temptations. Self-regulation involves making deliberate choices that align with one's goals, values, and long-term interests.

THE COMPONENTS OF SELF-REGULATION

Self-regulation encompasses several key components:

- **Emotional Regulation:** The ability to recognize, understand, and manage emotions. This involves not letting strong emotions dictate impulsive reactions.
- **Impulse Control:** The capacity to resist immediate gratification in favor of long-term goals. It entails resisting impulsive behaviors or decisions.
- **Behavioral Control:** The skill of consciously choosing behaviors that align with one's values and objectives, even when faced with external pressures or temptations.
- **Self-motivation:** The drive to persist in pursuing goals and tasks, especially when challenging or requiring sustained effort.

TECHNIQUES FOR IMPROVING SELF-REGULATION

1. Mindfulness Meditation

Mindfulness meditation is a powerful practice that enhances self-regulation by promoting emotional awareness and impulse control. People can learn to observe their thoughts and emotions without reacting hastily by practicing mindfulness. This heightened awareness empowers them to make more deliberate behavior and response choices.

2. Cognitive-Behavioral Therapy (CBT)

CBT is a therapeutic strategy that aids people in recognizing and challenging harmful thought patterns and behaviors. By identifying and changing irrational beliefs or automatic negative thoughts, people can better control their reactions and impulses.

3. Goal Setting and Planning

Setting clear and specific goals and developing actionable plans to achieve them enhances self-regulation. Individuals with a well-defined roadmap are more likely to stay focused and resist distractions or impulsive actions that deviate from their goals.

4. Time Management

Self-regulation includes effective time management as a critical component. It involves prioritizing tasks, setting boundaries, and allocating time for important activities. By managing their time efficiently, individuals can reduce stress and improve their ability to make intentional choices.

5. Stress Reduction Techniques

Stress can undermine self-regulation, leading to impulsive behaviors. People can manage stress and maintain self-control by using methods like deep breathing, progressive muscle relaxation, and mindfulness-based stress reduction.

THE ROLE OF SELF-DISCIPLINE IN SELF-REGULATION

Self-discipline is the backbone of self-regulation. It is the ability to control one's actions, resist temptations, and stay committed to long-term goals. Self-discipline involves making choices that prioritize future rewards over immediate gratification. Here's why self-discipline is integral to self-regulation:

1. Resisting Temptation

Self-discipline enables individuals to resist the allure of short-term pleasures that may undermine their long-term objectives. It helps them say no to distractions, Procrastination, or unhealthy habits.

2. Overcoming Procrastination

Procrastination is a common challenge that hinders self-regulation. Self-discipline empowers individuals to overcome Procrastination by taking action, even when tasks seem daunting or less enjoyable.

3. Consistency

Consistency is a hallmark of self-discipline. When individuals have self-discipline, they can consistently follow through on their commitments and obligations. This reliability builds trust and reliability in the eyes of others.

4. Building Habits

Self-discipline plays a crucial role in habit formation. It enables individuals to establish positive routines and maintain them over time. With self-discipline, new habits become ingrained and contribute to self-regulation.

5. Emotional Control

Self-discipline aids in emotional regulation by allowing individuals to manage their reactions to emotional triggers. Instead of succumbing to emotional outbursts, self-discipline helps individuals respond calmly and thoughtfully.

CULTIVATING SELF-REGULATION IN LEADERSHIP

In the context of leadership, self-regulation is essential for making sound decisions, maintaining composure in high-pressure situations, and setting an example for others. Leaders who practice self-regulation are better equipped to manage conflicts, adapt to change, and uphold ethical standards. They can also inspire their teams through their consistent actions and disciplined approach.

CONCLUSION

Self-regulation is vital to self-leadership—a skill that underpins effective leadership and creates a winning culture. Individuals can take charge of their impulses, emotions, and behaviors by understanding self-regulation and employing techniques to enhance it. Self-discipline, in particular, plays a central role in self-regulation, enabling individuals to resist temptations, stay committed to their goals, and maintain control over their actions. In the chapters ahead, we will continue exploring the multifaceted aspects of self-leadership and how they contribute to effective leadership and developing winning cultures within organizations.

CHAPTER 9
THE POWER OF SELF-MOTIVATION

As we continue our exploration of self-leadership, we turn our attention to another pivotal aspect—self-motivation. In this chapter, we will delve into the significance of self-motivation in self-leadership, explore techniques for enhancing self-motivation, and unravel the integral role of goal setting in fueling one's internal drive.

Defining Self-Motivation

Self-motivation, within self-leadership, refers to the drive and determination to pursue goals and objectives with enthusiasm and persistence. It is the engine that propels individuals forward, even when faced with challenges or obstacles. Self-motivation is not reliant on external rewards or incentives; instead, it emanates from an intrinsic desire to achieve and excel.

THE SIGNIFICANCE OF SELF-MOTIVATION

- **Sustaining Commitment:** Self-motivation enables individuals to stay committed to their goals over the long haul. When motivation comes from within, individuals are less likely to be deterred by setbacks or distractions.
- **Resilience:** Self-motivated individuals exhibit greater resilience in adversity. They remain upbeat even in trying circumstances and see setbacks as chances for improvement.
- **Initiative:** Self-motivation empowers individuals to take initiative and seize opportunities. They do not wait for external directives; instead, they proactively identify areas for improvement and innovation.
- **Leadership Example:** Self-motivated individuals lead by example, inspiring those around them with their dedication, work ethic, and unwavering commitment to their goals.

TECHNIQUES FOR IMPROVING SELF-MOTIVATION

1. Clarify your Goals

Start by defining clear, specific, and meaningful goals. Clarifying your objectives gives you a sense of purpose and direction. Ensure that your goals align with your values and aspirations.

2. Break Goals into Smaller Steps

Divide larger goals into smaller, manageable steps. This approach makes the path to your goals less daunting and allows you to celebrate incremental achievements.

3. Visualize success

Visualization is a powerful technique for enhancing self-motivation. Close your eyes and vividly imagine yourself successfully achieving your goals. Visualizing your success can boost your confidence and determination.

4. Find Intrinsic Rewards

Identify the intrinsic rewards associated with your goals. Consider the personal satisfaction, fulfilment, and sense of accomplishment you will derive from achieving them. Cultivate a deep appreciation for these intrinsic rewards.

5. Create a Motivational Environment

Surround yourself with sources of motivation. This could include motivational quotes, success stories, or reminders of your goals. An environment that fosters motivation can inspire you daily.

6. Maintain a Positive Mindset

Cultivate an optimistic mindset. Avoid negative self-talk or self-doubt. Replace limiting beliefs with affirmations that reinforce your self-motivation.

THE ROLE OF GOAL-SETTING IN SELF-MOTIVATION

Setting SMART Goals

Effective goal setting is a cornerstone of self-motivation. When setting goals, consider the SMART criteria:

- Specific: Clearly define your goals. Vague goals are challenging to pursue.
- Measurable: Make sure your objectives can be measured or quantified. You can monitor your progress in this way.
- Set goals: Set goals that are difficult to achieve but doable. Unattainable objectives may cause frustration.
- Relevant: Your objectives ought to be in line with your values and long-term goals. They ought to have personal significance.

- Time-Bound: Establish a target date for completing your tasks. As a result, there is a sense of responsibility and urgency.

The Motivating Power of Goals

- Goals serve as the driving force behind self-motivation. Here's how they play a pivotal role:
- Direction: Goals provide a clear direction, helping you focus your efforts on specific outcomes.
- Measurement: Goals allow you to measure progress and assess your achievements, providing a sense of accomplishment.
- Challenge: Challenging goals ignite motivation. They inspire you to push beyond your comfort zone and strive for excellence.
- Commitment: Setting goals creates a commitment to follow through and achieve what you've set out to accomplish.
- Intrinsic Motivation: Goals often tap into intrinsic motivation—the desire to achieve personal fulfilment.

CULTIVATING SELF-MOTIVATION IN LEADERSHIP

Leaders who practice self-motivation are more likely

to achieve their own goals and inspire their teams. Here's how self-motivation contributes to effective leadership:

- Inspiring Others: Self-motivated leaders set an example for their teams, motivating others to take initiative and pursue excellence.
- Resilience: In times of adversity, self-motivated leaders remain steadfast, providing stability and reassurance to their teams.
- Innovation: Self-motivated leaders drive innovation by encouraging their teams to seek new solutions and opportunities.
- Adaptability: Self-motivated leaders are more adaptable, optimistic and determined, guiding their teams through change.

CONCLUSION

Self-motivation is the driving force that propels individuals to pursue goals and objectives. It is a key component of self-leadership, empowering individuals to stay committed, resilient, and proactive. Techniques such as clarifying goals, breaking them into smaller steps, visualizing success, finding intrinsic rewards, creating a motivational environment, and maintaining a positive mindset can enhance self-motivation.

Moreover, goal setting is vital in self-motivation, providing direction, measurement, challenge, commitment, and intrinsic motivation. As we progress in our exploration of self-leadership and its role in creating winning cultures and leading teams, keep in mind that self-motivation is not just an individual trait—it's a leadership quality that can inspire and empower those around you.

CHAPTER 10

THE SELF-LEADER'S GUIDE TO UNSHAKEABLE SELF-CONFIDENCE

In our journey through the intricacies of self-leadership, we arrive at a critical juncture— self-confidence. In this chapter, we will explore the pivotal role of self-confidence in self-leadership, delve into techniques for bolstering self-confidence, and examine how this attribute profoundly influences leadership effectiveness.

Understanding Self-Confidence

Self-confidence is a fundamental component of self-leadership, serving as the foundation for leadership effectiveness. It is the belief in one's abilities, competence, and worthiness. The assurance that you can face challenges, make choices, and accomplish your goals is how self-confidence appears.

THE SIGNIFICANCE OF SELF-CONFIDENCE

- **Empowerment:** Self-confidence empowers individuals to take the initiative and seize opportunities. It allows them to leave their comfort zones and venture into the unknown with poise.
- **Resilience:** Self-confident individuals are more resilient in facing setbacks and adversity. They view failures as temporary setbacks, not insurmountable obstacles.
- **Effective Decision-Making:** Self-confidence facilitates effective decision-making. When you trust your judgment and abilities, you can decide with conviction.
- **Influence:** Self-confidence enhances your ability to influence and inspire others. Confidence is magnetic, drawing people towards those who exude it.
- **Risk-Taking:** Self-confident individuals are more willing to take calculated risks. They understand that growth often requires stepping into the unknown.

TECHNIQUES FOR IMPROVING SELF-CONFIDENCE

1. Positive Self-Talk

The words you say to yourself matter. Replace self-doubt and criticism with positive affirmations and self-encouragement. Acknowledge your achievements and strengths regularly.

2. Visualization

Visualization is a powerful technique for building self-confidence. Visualize yourself successfully navigating challenges and achieving your goals. This mental rehearsal reinforces your belief in your capabilities.

3. Continuous Learning

Invest in your personal and professional development. Acquiring new knowledge and skills boosts your competence and, in turn, your self-confidence.

4. Set Achievable Goals

Setting and accomplishing small, achievable goals gradually builds your confidence. As you experience success, your belief in your abilities grows.

5. Embrace failure

Failure is not a reflection of your worth. Accept

setbacks as chances to improve and learn. Each setback can be a stepping stone toward greater self-confidence.

6. Seek feedback

Solicit feedback from trusted colleagues, mentors, or coaches. Constructive feedback can highlight your strengths and areas for improvement, reinforcing your self-awareness and confidence.

THE IMPACT OF SELF-CONFIDENCE ON LEADERSHIP EFFECTIVENESS

1. Inspiring Trust

Self-confident leaders inspire trust among their teams. When you believe in yourself, others are more likely to believe in you. Trust is the foundation of strong leadership.

2. Decision-Making

Leaders with self-confidence make decisions with conviction. They weigh options, make choices, and stand by them. This decisiveness fosters clarity and direction within teams.

3. Communication

Self-confident leaders communicate effectively and

assertively. They convey their ideas, expectations, and vision clearly, inspiring alignment and commitment among team members.

4. Resilience

In the face of challenges and setbacks, self-confident leaders remain resilient. They lead by example, demonstrating that failures are temporary and perseverance is key to success.

5. Risk-Taking

Confident leaders are more willing to take calculated risks. They understand that innovation and growth often require venturing into the unknown.

CULTIVATING SELF-CONFIDENCE IN LEADERSHIP

Leaders can actively cultivate self-confidence within themselves and their teams:

- Encourage Self-Discovery: Foster an environment where team members can discover their strengths and interests. This self-discovery can boost self-confidence.
- Provide Opportunities: Offer opportunities for team members to take on new challenges

and responsibilities. Please encourage them to stretch their capabilities and embrace growth.

- Celebrate Achievements: Celebrate both individual and team achievements. Recognize and acknowledge contributions, reinforcing a sense of competence and confidence.
- Feedback and Coaching: Provide constructive feedback and coaching to help team members improve and grow. Positive guidance can enhance self-confidence.

CONCLUSION

Self-confidence is the cornerstone of self-leadership —a vital attribute that empowers individuals to take charge of their destinies, overcome challenges, and achieve their goals. Techniques such as positive self-talk, visualization, continuous learning, goal setting, embracing failure, and seeking feedback can enhance self-confidence.

Moreover, self-confidence profoundly impacts leadership effectiveness. Confident leaders inspire trust, make sound decisions, communicate effectively, exhibit resilience, and embrace risk-taking. They set the tone for a winning culture within their organizations, motivating others to believe in themselves and reach new heights of success. As we continue our journey through self-leadership, remember that self-confidence is not just a trait; It's a talent that can be developed and fostered, propelling you towards greater leadership success and creating winning cultures.

CHAPTER 11

SELF-BELIEF- THE CATALYST OF SELF-LEADERSHIP

In our journey through self-leadership, we arrive at a pivotal juncture—the realm of self- belief. This chapter delves into the profound significance of self-belief in self-leadership, explores techniques to bolster one's self-belief, and uncovers the intimate connection between self-belief and resilience.

Understanding Self-Belief

Self-belief is the unwavering confidence in one's abilities, judgments, and potential. It is the bedrock upon which self-leadership is constructed, fueling one's capacity to make decisions, seize opportunities, and navigate challenges. Self-belief is the potent force that propels individuals to transcend their limitations and embrace their full potential.

THE SIGNIFICANCE OF SELF-BELIEF

- Empowerment: Self-belief empowers individuals to take control of their destinies. It serves as the driving force that propels them forward, even in the face of uncertainty or adversity.
- Courage: Self-belief encourages individuals to leave their comfort zones and embrace new challenges. It is the catalyst that enables them to conquer fear and self-doubt.
- Resilience: Self-belief fortifies individuals against setbacks and failures. It imbues them with the conviction that they possess the inner resources to bounce back from adversity.
- Innovation: Self-belief fosters a mindset of innovation and experimentation. It encourages individuals to explore uncharted territories and push the boundaries of their capabilities.
- Leadership: Self-belief is an essential trait of effective leaders. Leaders who exude self-

belief inspire confidence in their teams and serve as beacons of determination and purpose.

TECHNIQUES FOR IMPROVING SELF-BELIEF

1. Challenge Self-Doubt

Identify and challenge self-doubt when it arises. Question the validity of negative thoughts and beliefs. Are they based on facts or irrational fears? Consciously replace self-doubt with affirmations of self-belief.

2. Visualize success

Visualization is a powerful technique for enhancing self-belief. Close your eyes and mentally visualize accomplishing your objectives and getting past challenges. This mental rehearsal reinforces your confidence in your abilities.

3. Cultivate a Growth Mindset

Adopt a growth mindset in which you see obstacles and failures as chances for development and learning. Accept the idea that with commitment and effort, you can improve your skills.

4. Set and Achieve Goals

Set clear, achievable goals and work diligently to accomplish them. Each achievement reinforces your belief in your competence and capacity to succeed.

5. Seek Positive Role Models

Surround yourself with positive role models who exude self-belief. Observe their behaviors, attitudes, and resilience. Learn from their example and seek their guidance.

6. Constructive Self-Reflection

Regularly engage in self-reflection to assess your progress and acknowledge your accomplishments. Celebrate your successes, regardless of their scale.

THE RELATIONSHIP BETWEEN SELF-BELIEF AND RESILIENCE

The Resilience of Self-Belief

- Positive Outlook: Self-belief cultivates a positive outlook. When individuals believe in their ability to overcome challenges, setbacks are viewed as temporary obstacles, not impossible ones.
- Adaptability: Self-belief fosters adaptability. Resilient individuals navigate change gracefully, possessing the self-assurance to confront uncertainty and embrace new opportunities.
- Optimism: Self-belief fuels optimism. Optimistic individuals maintain their faith in a positive outcome, even when confronted with adversity. This optimism bolsters their resilience.
- Problem-solving: Resilient individuals exhibit robust problem-solving skills. They approach challenges with confidence, exploring solutions and alternatives with determination.

BUILDING RESILIENCE THROUGH SELF-BELIEF

- Failure as Growth: Self-belief reframes failure as an integral part of growth. Rather than viewing failures as defeats, individuals with self-belief see them as stepping stones toward improvement.
- Self-Compassion: Self-belief encourages self-compassion. Resilient individuals treat themselves with kindness and understanding, even in the face of setbacks.
- Emotional Regulation: Self-belief enhances emotional regulation. Resilient individuals manage stress and adversity effectively, maintaining composure and a positive attitude.
- Adversity as Opportunity: Self-belief transforms adversity into opportunity. Resilient individuals embrace challenges as chances to test their mettle and expand their horizons.

CULTIVATING SELF-BELIEF IN LEADERSHIP

Leaders can actively cultivate self-belief within themselves and their teams:

- Inspiring Vision: Paint a compelling vision for your team's future. A powerful vision kindles self-belief, as team members see themselves contributing to something meaningful.

- Recognition: Celebrate and acknowledge both team and individual accomplishments.
- Acknowledgment fosters self-belief by reinforcing a sense of competence and value.
- Supportive Environment: Foster a supportive and empowering environment where team members feel safe to voice their ideas and take calculated risks. Such an environment nurtures self-belief.
- Mentorship and Coaching: Provide mentorship and coaching to help team members develop their skills and self-belief. Constructive feedback and guidance can be transformative.

CONCLUSION

Self-belief is the bedrock of self-leadership—a potent force that empowers individuals to embrace their potential, conquer challenges, and achieve their goals. Techniques such as challenging self-doubt, visualization, cultivating a growth mindset, setting and achieving goals, seeking positive role models, and engaging in constructive self-reflection can enhance self-belief.

Moreover, self-belief is intimately tied to resilience. Resilient individuals, fortified by self-belief, approach adversity with optimism, adaptability, and problem-solving skills. As we progress through self-leadership and the creation of winning cultures, remember that self-belief is not merely an attribute; it's a dynamic force that propels individuals and teams toward unprecedented success and fulfilment.

CHAPTER 12
SELF-EFFICACY

In exploring self-leadership, we delve into a profound aspect—self-efficacy. This chapter unfolds the significance of self-efficacy in self-leadership, illuminates techniques for enhancing it, and unveils its profound impact on leadership effectiveness.

Defining Self-Efficacy

The confidence in one's capacity to carry out particular tasks, achieve objectives, and deal with difficulties is known as self-efficacy. It is not a global assessment of one's self-worth but a domain-specific evaluation of competence. Self-efficacy is context-dependent, meaning it varies across different situations and tasks.

THE SIGNIFICANCE OF SELF-EFFICACY

- **Motivation**: Self-efficacy fuels motivation. Individuals who believe in their capabilities are morc likely to set ambitious goals and persevere.
- **Performance:** Self-efficacy influences performance. Those with high self-efficacy approach tasks more confidently and are more likely to succeed.
- **Resilience:** Self-efficacy enhances resilience. It fortifies individuals against setbacks and failures, as they view challenges as opportunities to apply their skills and knowledge.
- **Decision-Making:** Self-efficacy impacts decision-making. Individuals with high self-efficacy are more inclined to make choices that align with their goals and aspirations.
- **Innovation:** Self-efficacy fosters innovation. Those who believe in their problem- solving

abilities are likelier to explore new solutions and embrace creativity.

TECHNIQUES FOR IMPROVING SELF-EFFICACY

1. Mastery Experiences

The most potent way to enhance self-efficacy is through mastery experiences—completing tasks or achieving goals. Each success reinforces belief in one's capabilities. Start with small, achievable tasks and gradually tackle more challenging ones.

2. Vicarious Learning

Observing others who have succeeded in similar tasks can boost self-efficacy. Learn from the experiences of role models or mentors. Their accomplishments serve as an inspiration and a guide.

3. Social Persuasion

Positive feedback and encouragement from others can bolster self-efficacy. Seek support and constructive feedback from colleagues, mentors, or coaches. Their belief in your abilities can fortify your self-efficacy.

4. Emotional and Physiological States

Manage emotional and physiological states effectively. Anxiety and stress can erode self- efficacy, while a calm and focused mindset enhances it. Techniques such as mindfulness, relaxation, and stress management can be beneficial.

5. Cognitive Appraisal

Challenge and reframe self-limiting beliefs. Replace negative self-talk with affirmations of self-efficacy. Cultivate a growth mindset wherein you view challenges as opportunities for learning and growth.

6. Goal setting

Set clear and challenging goals. As you accomplish these goals, your self-efficacy will grow. Make certain that your objectives are SMART—specific, measurable, achievable, relevant, and time-bound.

THE IMPACT OF SELF-EFFICACY ON LEADERSHIP EFFECTIVENESS

1. Confidence in Decision-Making

Leaders with high self-efficacy exhibit confidence in their decision-making. They trust their judgment and are likelier to make bold and well-informed choices.

2. Motivating Teams

Self-efficacious leaders inspire and motivate their teams. Their belief in their capabilities is contagious, encouraging team members to believe in themselves and their collective potential.

3. Resilience

Leaders with strong self-efficacy are resilient in the face of adversity. They maintain composure, navigate challenges with determination, and lead by example.

4. Innovative Leadership

Self-efficacious leaders are more inclined to embrace innovation. They encourage their teams to explore new solutions and approaches, fostering a culture of creativity.

5. Empowering Others

Leaders with high self-efficacy empower their teams. They provide autonomy and support, enabling team members to take responsibility for their work and effectively contribute.

CULTIVATING SELF-EFFICACY IN LEADERSHIP

Leaders can actively cultivate self-efficacy within themselves and their teams:

- Set Stretch Goals: Encourage team members to set ambitious but achievable goals. Provide opportunities for them to stretch their capabilities and realize their potential.
- Acknowledge Efforts: Recognize and celebrate individual and team efforts. Acknowledgment reinforces self-efficacy by highlighting competence and value.
- Provide Feedback: Offer constructive feedback and guidance to help team members learn and grow. Positive feedback reinforces belief in one's capabilities.
- Create a Safe Environment: Encourage the creation of a safe and encouraging environment where team members feel

confident taking calculated risks and looking for new solutions.

CONCLUSION

Self-efficacy is a dynamic force in self-leadership—a belief in one's abilities to perform tasks, achieve goals, and overcome challenges. Techniques such as mastery experiences, vicarious learning, social persuasion, managing emotional and physiological states, cognitive appraisal, and goal setting can enhance self-efficacy.

Moreover, self-efficacy significantly impacts leadership effectiveness. Confident leaders make bold decisions, motivate their teams, exhibit resilience, foster innovation, and empower others. As we navigate self-leadership and the creation of winning cultures, Do not forget that self-efficacy is a skill that can be developed and utilized, unlocking untapped leadership potential and driving teams towards unprecedented success.

CHAPTER 13
SELF-MANAGEMENT

In our ongoing exploration of self-leadership, we arrive at a fundamental aspect—self- management. This chapter unveils the crucial role of self-management in self- leadership, provides techniques for enhancing it, and emphasizes the significance of prioritization in effective self-management.

Defining Self-Management

Self-management is effectively controlling and regulating one's thoughts, emotions, behaviors, and actions. It is the cornerstone of self-leadership, enabling individuals to navigate their inner world and external challenges with poise and intention.

THE SIGNIFICANCE OF SELF-MANAGEMENT

- **Emotional Regulation:** Self-management empowers individuals to regulate their emotions, maintaining composure even in emotionally charged situations.
- **Time Management:** Effective self-management includes time management. It enables individuals to allocate their time wisely, focusing on tasks that align with their goals and priorities.
- **Stress Reduction**: Self-management mitigates stress. It equips individuals with tools to manage stressors, preventing them from overwhelming the mind and body.
- **Productivity:** Effective self-management enhances productivity. It enables individuals to stay focused, efficiently use their time, and accomplish tasks effectively.
- **Adaptability:** Self-management fosters adaptability. It equips individuals with the resilience to navigate change and uncertainty gracefully.

TECHNIQUES FOR IMPROVING SELF-MANAGEMENT

1. Self-Awareness

Begin with self-awareness. Recognize your emotional triggers, time-wasting habits, and stressors. Self-awareness is the first step in self-management.

2. Goal Setting

Set clear, specific, and achievable goals. Goals provide direction and purpose, helping you prioritize your efforts.

3. Time Management

Master the art of time management. Use techniques like the Pomodoro Technique, Eisenhower Matrix, or time-blocking to allocate your time effectively.

4. Stress Management

Develop stress-management techniques that work for you. This could include mindfulness, meditation, exercise, or deep breathing exercises.

5. Emotional Regulation

Learn to recognize and manage your emotions. Practice emotional intelligence by understanding the emotions of others as well.

6. Decision-Making

Enhance your decision-making skills. Use tools like decision matrices or pros and cons lists to make informed choices.

7. Prioritization

Prioritize tasks and responsibilities based on their importance and urgency. The Eisenhower Matrix (Quadrant II) is useful for this purpose.

THE IMPORTANCE OF PRIORITIZATION IN SELF-MANAGEMENT

1. Identifying Key Goals

Prioritization helps individuals identify their most important goals and objectives. It forces a focus on what truly matters.

2. Time Allocation

Effective self-management includes allocating time and resources to high-priority tasks. Prioritization ensures that the most critical activities receive adequate attention.

3. Reducing Overwhelm

Prioritization reduces overwhelm. When individuals attempt to tackle too many tasks simultaneously, stress and burnout can result. Prioritization prevents this by streamlining efforts.

4. Enhancing productivity

Prioritization boosts productivity. It enables individuals to complete important tasks efficiently, reducing the time and energy expended on less critical activities.

5. Strategic Decision-Making

Prioritization aids in strategic decision-making. It ensures that decisions align with overarching goals and objectives.

CULTIVATING SELF-MANAGEMENT IN LEADERSHIP

Leaders can actively cultivate self-management within themselves and their teams:

- Lead by Example: Demonstrate effective self-management through your actions and behaviors. Show your team the benefits of emotional regulation, time management, and stress reduction.
- Provide Resources: Offer resources and training in self-management techniques. Equip your team with the tools they need to enhance their self-management skills.
- Encourage Self-Care: Promote self-care practices within your team. Emphasize the importance of work-life balance and stress management.
- Set Clear Expectations: Communicate expectations and priorities to your team. Ensure everyone understands the most important tasks and goals.

CONCLUSION

Self-management is the linchpin of self-leadership—a vital skill enabling individuals to control their thoughts, emotions, behaviors, and actions effectively. Self-awareness, goal setting, time management, stress management, emotional regulation, decision-making, and prioritization can enhance self-management.

Moreover, self-management significantly influences leadership effectiveness. Leaders who excel in self-management lead by example, provide resources for skill development, promote self-care, and set clear expectations for their teams. As we continue our journey in self-leadership and creating winning cultures, remember that self-management is not a static trait; it's a dynamic skill that can be honed and refined, propelling individuals and teams toward unparalleled success and fulfilment.

CHAPTER 14
SELF-DEVELOPMENT

In our journey through self-leadership, we arrive at a pivotal juncture—self-development. This chapter unravels the paramount importance of self-development in self-leadership, offers techniques for continuous self-improvement, and underscores the indispensable role of ongoing learning in this endeavor.

Defining Self-Development

Self-development is the intentional and continuous process of enhancing one's knowledge, skills, abilities, and personal qualities. It is the bedrock upon which self-leadership thrives, enabling individuals to evolve, adapt, and lead with ever-growing effectiveness.

The Significance of Self-Development

Adaptability: Self-development fosters adaptability. It equips individuals to embrace change and navigate uncertainty with agility.

- **Growth:** Self-development propels personal and professional growth. It empowers individuals to stretch their capabilities and reach new heights of achievement.
- **Innovation:** Self-development cultivates innovative thinking. Continuous learning and improvement spark creativity, leading to innovative solutions and approaches.
- **Resilience:** Self-development enhances resilience. Individuals who invest in their development are better equipped to bounce back from setbacks and failures.
- **Leadership Evolution:** Effective self-leadership necessitates ongoing self-development. Leaders must continually

refine their skills and knowledge to lead effectively.

TECHNIQUES FOR ONGOING SELF-DEVELOPMENT

1. Goal Setting

Set clear and specific development goals. These goals can encompass various areas, such as professional skills, personal growth, or leadership competencies.

2. Reflective Practice

Regularly engage in reflective practice. Self-reflection allows individuals to assess their progress, determine where they can improve and change their tactics accordingly.

3. Seek feedback

Solicit feedback from colleagues, mentors, or coaches. Constructive feedback provides insights into areas for development and guides the self-improvement process.

4. Continuous Learning

Embrace continuous learning. Stay curious and open-minded, seeking opportunities to acquire new knowledge and skills.

5. Networking

Build a network of peers, mentors, and experts. Networking exposes individuals to diverse perspectives and knowledge, fostering growth and development.

6. Mentorship and Coaching

Engage in mentorship and coaching relationships. Mentors and coaches provide guidance, support, and expertise, accelerating self-development.

THE ROLE OF CONTINUOUS LEARNING IN SELF-DEVELOPMENT

1. Acquiring New Skills

Continuous learning enables individuals to acquire new skills and competencies. These skills can be applied personally and professionally, enhancing one's capabilities.

2. Staying Relevant

In a rapidly changing world, continuous learning ensures individuals stay relevant. It equips them with up-to-date knowledge and insights that are vital for success.

3. Expanding Perspectives

Learning exposes individuals to new ideas and perspectives. This broader outlook enhances creativity and innovative thinking.

4. Problem-Solving

Continuous learning hones problem-solving abilities. Well-informed individuals can approach challenges with greater efficacy.

5. Career Advancement

Ongoing learning is essential for career advancement. It positions individuals as valuable assets to their organizations and opens doors to new opportunities.

CULTIVATING SELF-DEVELOPMENT IN LEADERSHIP

Leaders can actively cultivate self-development within themselves and their teams:

- Lead by Example: Demonstrate a commitment to self-development through your actions. Share your experiences and encourage team members to engage in self-improvement.
- Provide Resources: Offer resources, such as books, courses, or workshops, to support self-development efforts within your team.
- Encourage Feedback: Foster a culture of constructive feedback. Encourage team members to seek feedback and use it for growth.
- Recognize Achievements: Recognize and celebrate individual and team achievements related to self-development. Acknowledgment reinforces the value of continuous improvement.

CONCLUSION

Self-development is the lifeblood of self-leadership—a relentless pursuit of growth, knowledge, and improvement. Techniques such as goal setting, reflective practice, seeking feedback, continuous learning, networking, and mentorship can fuel self-development.

Moreover, continuous learning is the linchpin of self-development. It equips individuals with new skills, keeps them relevant, broadens their perspectives, enhances problem-solving abilities, and paves the path for career advancement. As we continue our journey in self-leadership and creating winning cultures, remember that self-development is not a destination; it's an ongoing journey that fuels personal and organizational success, enabling individuals and teams to thrive in an ever-evolving world.

CHAPTER 15
SELF-CARE

In exploring self-leadership, we've arrived at a crucial juncture—self-care. This chapter illuminates the paramount importance of self-care in self-leadership, offers techniques for enhancing it, and underscores the profound relationship between self-care and leadership effectiveness.

Defining Self-Care

Self-care is deliberately tending to one's physical, emotional, and mental well-being. It is the bedrock upon which self-leadership thrives, enabling individuals to sustain their vitality, resilience, and effectiveness.

THE SIGNIFICANCE OF SELF-CARE

- **Resilience:** Self-care fosters resilience. It equips individuals with the capacity to bounce back from adversity and navigate challenging situations with poise.
- **Physical Health:** Self-care promotes physical health. It includes practices like exercise, nutrition, and adequate sleep, which are fundamental for overall well-being.
- **Emotional Regulation:** Self-care supports emotional regulation. Engaging in self-soothing activities reduces stress and anxiety, fostering emotional stability.
- **Mental Clarity:** Self-care enhances mental clarity. Taking breaks and engaging in relaxation techniques rejuvenates the mind, enabling sharper focus and decision-making.
- **Preventing Burnout:** Self-care prevents burnout. It ensures that individuals maintain a healthy work-life balance, protecting them from exhaustion and overwhelm.

TECHNIQUES FOR IMPROVING SELF-CARE

1. Prioritize rest

Make rest and sleep a priority. Ensure you sleep well each night to recharge your body and mind.

2. Exercise Regularly

Incorporate regular physical activity into your routine. Exercise releases endorphins, reducing stress and enhancing mood.

3. Nutrition

Maintain a balanced diet. Proper nutrition provides the energy and nutrients your body needs to function optimally.

4. Mindfulness and Meditation

Practice mindfulness and meditation. These techniques promote emotional regulation, reduce stress, and enhance mental clarity.

5. Boundaries

Set clear boundaries between work and personal life. Protect your time and energy by limiting work-related tasks during non-work hours.

6. Hobbies and Interests

Engage in hobbies and activities you enjoy. These pursuits provide a sense of fulfilment and relaxation.

Don't hesitate to seek support from friends, family, or a therapist. Talking about your concerns can provide emotional relief.

THE RELATIONSHIP BETWEEN SELF-CARE AND LEADERSHIP EFFECTIVENESS

1. Resilience

Leaders who practice self-care exhibit greater resilience. They are better equipped to face adversity and maintain composure during challenging times.

2. Emotional Intelligence

Self-care enhances emotional intelligence. Leaders who practice self-regulation and emotional regulation are more effective in understanding and managing their own emotions and those of their teams.

3. Decision-Making

Clear, rested minds make better decisions. Leaders who prioritize self-care are more likely to make sound, well-considered choices.

4. Empathy and Compassion

Self-care fosters empathy and compassion. Leaders who care for their well-being are more inclined to empathize with the needs and concerns of their team members.

5. Role Modeling

Leaders who practice self-care set a positive example for their teams. They demonstrate the importance of balance and well-being, encouraging their team members to do the same.

CULTIVATING SELF-CARE IN LEADERSHIP

Leaders can actively cultivate self-care within themselves and their teams:

- Lead by Example: Demonstrate the importance of self-care through your actions. Prioritize your well-being and encourage team members to do the same.
- Create a Supportive Environment: Develop a self-care culture within your company. Encourage your staff to set boundaries, take breaks, and seek help.
- Provide Resources: Offer resources such as wellness programs, mental health support, and access to fitness facilities to support self-care efforts within your team.
- Promote Work-Life Balance: Encourage work-life balance by setting realistic expectations and respecting non-work hours. Promote flexible work arrangements when feasible.

CONCLUSION

Self-care is the cornerstone of self-leadership—a practice that nurtures physical, emotional, and mental well-being. Techniques such as prioritizing rest, regular exercise, proper nutrition, mindfulness, setting boundaries, engaging in hobbies, and seeking support can fuel self-care.

Moreover, self-care profoundly impacts leadership effectiveness. Leaders who prioritize self-care exhibit resilience, emotional intelligence, sound decision-making, empathy, and compassion. As we continue our journey in self-leadership and creating winning cultures, remember that self-care is not a luxury; it's an essential practice that bolsters personal and organizational success, enabling individuals and teams to thrive in an ever-demanding world.

CHAPTER 16
SELF-LEADERSHIP - THE CATALYST FOR SUCCESS

As we conclude our journey through the realms of self-leadership, it is fitting to reflect upon its profound power, its transformative impact on personal and professional success, and the enduring recommendations for ongoing self-leadership development.

Defining Self-Leadership

Self-leadership is taking control of one's thoughts, emotions, behaviors, and actions to navigate life with intention, purpose, and effectiveness. It is a dynamic force that empowers individuals to chart their course, regardless of their position or title.

THE MULTIFACETED NATURE OF SELF-LEADERSHIP

- **Self-Awareness:** Self-leadership involves self-awareness—an understanding of one's strengths, weaknesses, values, and aspirations.
- **Self-Regulation**: It extends to self-regulation, where individuals harness their emotions and behaviors, ensuring alignment with their goals and values.
- **Self-Motivation:** Self-leadership involves self-motivation—the drive to set and achieve meaningful goals, even in the face of challenges.
- **Self-Confidence:** Confidence in one's abilities is pivotal. Self-leadership bolsters self-confidence, enabling individuals to take calculated risks and tackle new opportunities.
- **Self-Belief:** Self-leadership fosters self-belief—the unwavering faith in one's potential, even when confronted with adversity.

- **Self-Efficacy:** Finally, self-leadership nurtures self-efficacy, the belief in one's competence to navigate and succeed in various life domains.

THE IMPACT OF SELF-LEADERSHIP ON PERSONAL AND PROFESSIONAL SUCCESS

1. Personal Fulfilment

Self-leadership is a pathway to personal fulfilment. It gives people the skills they need to follow their passions, set and accomplish meaningful goals, and live lives that are consistent with their values.

2. Resilience

Self-leadership fosters resilience. It empowers individuals to bounce back from setbacks, navigate challenges with composure, and view adversity as an opportunity for growth.

3. Emotional Intelligence

Self-leadership enhances emotional intelligence. It enables people to comprehend and control their emotions as well as those of others, promoting fruitful interpersonal interactions.

4. Empathy

Empathy flourishes in the realm of self-leadership. Leaders who practice self-awareness and emotional regulation are better equipped to empathize with the experiences and emotions of their team members.

5. Decision-Making

Clear, focused minds make sound decisions. Self-leadership cultivates effective decision-making, ensuring choices align with personal and organizational goals.

6. Goal Attainment

Self-leadership propels goal attainment. Individuals who practice self-motivation and self-regulation are more likely to set high standards for themselves and devote themselves to achieving them.

FINAL THOUGHTS AND RECOMMENDATIONS FOR ONGOING SELF-LEADERSHIP DEVELOPMENT

1. Cultivate Self-Awareness

The journey of self-leadership commences with self-awareness. Continually explore your values, strengths, weaknesses, and aspirations. Regularly engage in self-reflection to refine your understanding of yourself.

2. Embrace Continuous Learning

Self-leadership is an evolving process. Embrace continuous learning to stay current and relevant. Explore new ideas, seek diverse perspectives, and remain open to growth opportunities.

3. Prioritize Self-Care

Self-care is non-negotiable. Prioritize your physical, emotional, and mental well-being. Make rest, exercise, nutrition, and relaxation integral to your routine.

4. Seek feedback

Feedback is a valuable resource for growth. Actively

seek feedback from trusted colleagues, mentors, or coaches. Use feedback as a tool for self-improvement.

5. Set Clear Goals

Set clear, specific, and challenging goals. Goals provide direction and purpose, guiding your actions and decisions. Review your goals frequently and make necessary adjustments.

6. Cultivate resilience

Resilience is a cornerstone of self-leadership. Develop resilience by practicing adaptability, seeing setbacks as opportunities for growth, and keeping a positive outlook.

7. Lead by Example

As a leader, lead by example. Demonstrate the principles of self-leadership through your actions and behaviors. Inspire your team to embark on their journeys of self-discovery and growth.

8. Foster a Culture of Self-Leadership

Within your organization or team, foster a culture of self-leadership. Encourage colleagues to take ownership of their growth and well-being. Provide resources and support for their development.

CONCLUSION

Self-leadership is the linchpin of personal and professional success—a dynamic force that empowers individuals to navigate life with intention, purpose, and effectiveness. It encompasses self-awareness, self-regulation, self-motivation, self-confidence, self-belief, and self-efficacy.

The impact of self-leadership extends to personal

fulfilment, resilience, emotional intelligence, empathy, effective decision-making, and goal attainment. It is a practice that transcends titles and positions, enabling individuals to thrive in a rapidly evolving world.

As we conclude this journey, remember that self-leadership is a lifelong pursuit. Embrace it as a continuous journey of self-discovery, growth, and fulfilment. By practicing self-leadership, you empower yourself to lead with authenticity, purpose, and unwavering effectiveness and inspire others to do the same. The power of self-leadership lies within you, waiting to be harnessed for the betterment of yourself and those you lead.

The M Series consultants and contributors

Dr. Pat Ivey
Dr. Frankie Collins
Greg. "Mayor" Jones
Peter Gilliam
Greg Skeen
David Shird
Gabe Jackson
Martin Lee
Asher Touchua
Brian Keith
Shedrich Webster

ABOUT THE AUTHOR

Barry Nembhard is a renowned executive coach, author, and advocate known for his transformative work in leadership development and personal growth. With over 20 years of experience in human resources and executive leadership, he has guided numerous individuals and organizations towards unparalleled success.

Barry Nembhard's journey to coaching excellence began during his time as a collegiate athlete, where he honed his skills in teamwork, discipline, and resilience. Drawing from his athletic background, he seamlessly transitioned into the corporate world, serving as a trusted HR executive for two decades. His strategic insights and people-centric approach have helped shape thriving workplace cultures and empowered employees to reach their full potential. Beyond his corporate endeavors, Barry Nembhard is a dedicated advocate for families and children within the family court system.

His commitment to justice and support for vulnerable populations has made a lasting impact on the lives of many, inspiring hope and fostering positive change within communities.

As a passionate mentor and coach, Barry Nembhard has dedicated his time to nurturing young talents as an AAU coach, instilling values of teamwork, perseverance, and leadership in the next generation. His unwavering dedication to youth development has laid the foundation for countless individuals to excel both on and off the court. In addition to his coaching and advocacy work, Barry Nembhard has served as a trusted small business consultant for two decades, guiding entrepreneurs and organizations towards sustainable growth and success. His strategic guidance and entrepreneurial acumen have been instrumental in helping businesses thrive in competitive markets.

Outside of his professional endeavors, Barry Nembhard is a nature enthusiast and lover of the outdoors. He finds solace and inspiration in the beauty of the natural world, often incorporating its teachings into his coaching philosophy to foster holistic well-being and personal growth.

Barry Nembhard's multifaceted background, unwavering dedication to empowerment, and passion for fostering positive change have solidified his reputation as a transformative leader and a beacon of inspiration in the world of executive coaching.